Rebooting Astronomy Instruction with Collaborative Learning

Table of Contents

Chapter 1. Introduction

Special Report: Rebooting Astronomy Instruction with Collaborative Learning

Dive deep into an exciting, cutting-edge transformation in astronomy instruction, where the cosmos gets a fresh, collaborative spin! In this special report, we illuminate how the age-old science of observing celestial bodies is getting a vibrant shake-up, embracing collaborative learning approaches. Our experts untangle the complex threads of these innovative strategies in an accessible narrative that will captivate educators, students, and astronomy enthusiasts alike. No need for a scientific degree to appreciate how these changes can empower students, foster teamwork, and ignite passion for the universe. Be prepared to be swept off your feet and into the captivating world of modern astronomy instruction—a world where learning becomes a shared journey, as limitless and fascinating as the cosmos. Secure your copy of our Special Report today and join us on this exciting trek into the future of astronomy education!

Chapter 2. Reimagining Astronomy Education: An Introduction

The field of astronomy instruction is undergoing a revolution, or perhaps more accurately, an evolution. The processes and methodologies with which we introduce students to the universe are being reimagined and reconstructed. Traditional instructional methods are making way for a dynamic, more hands-on and collaborative approach to teaching astronomy. Breaking down the walls of isolation, we are entering an era where learning is viewed as a collective journey, much like the universe itself, vast, interconnected, and continuously expanding.

2.1. A New Dawn in Astronomy Education

Astronomy has long been a field of study that prides itself in eliciting a sense of mystery, adventure, and, to a certain extent, romanticism. The ethereal beauty of celestial bodies, the infinite expanses of galaxies, and the profound and humbling insignificance of our existence in the grand cosmic play only compel us more to uncover the secrets that lie beyond our earthly bonds. However, pedagogy in this field has not always been as enchanting or as engaging. Traditional methods can often be isolating, focusing more on individual understanding and rote learning.

Today, we are rediscovering the essence of teaching astronomy and the importance of adopting a collaborative paradigm. This shift is motivated by the recognition that learning does not occur in a silo. Our knowledge and understanding are a product of our interactions, discussions, and collaborations. Information is absorbed more effectively when it becomes part of a collective experience and is subjected to communal dialogue and debate. The interplay of different perspectives, interpretations, and understandings enrich the learning process.

2.2. Collaborative Learning: Breaking Down the Walls

Imagine the difference between a student reading a textbook description of a black hole and a group of students discussing and constructing their understanding of black holes through a collaborative project. The second scenario promotes not only a deeper understanding of the topic but it nurtures a plethora of skills such as teamwork, communication, critical thinking, and problem-solving. These are skills that are crucial for success in our interconnected, globalized world - and they are not exclusively tied to astronomy.

Collaborative learning does not merely incorporate teamwork into educational practices; it revolutionizes the classroom dynamic. Under this approach, teachers are not the sole sources of information; instead, they serve a facilitative role, guiding students through the learning experience. A greater emphasis is placed on student interaction, group activities, and communal problem solving.

2.3. Embracing Technology

The past two decades have seen an unprecedented surge in technological advancements. Today, we have technology literally at our fingertips, that can bring the furthest galaxies to our desktops, and this is a game-changer for astronomy education. Virtual reality environments, interactive star maps, and digital planetariums have not only redefined the student learning experience but also facilitated a shift towards interactive and collaborative learning.

Embracing these technologies in the classroom allows for a different type of learning - an immersive learning adventure where students can interact directly with the material. They can explore simulated environments, manipulate celestial bodies, and interact with each other in these artificial environments. This opens up a whole new frontier in astronomy education, setting the stage for more engaging and effective learning experiences.

2.4. Constructing Concepts: The Role of Interactive Projects

Projects that require teamwork and shared responsibility are central to the collaborative learning model. They challenge learners to extend beyond their comfort zones and work together towards a common goal. In astronomy education, these projects often revolve around the construction of models, simulations, and visual representations of celestial phenomenons using technological tools.

For instance, a project might involve creating a three-dimensional model of a solar system using software or constructing a night sky map of various constellations. Another project might be to design, conduct, and analyze an experiment related to gravitational forces via a physics simulation software. Here, the learning extends beyond mere theoretical understanding. It incorporates application, rationalization, interpretation, and innovation - fostering a holistic grasp of astronomical concepts.

2.5. Future Prospects

Today's advancements in collaborative learning strategies herald a bright future for astronomy education. Moving forward, expect to see more engaging, interactive classrooms where dialogue, debate, and discussion are at the heart of the learning experience. We will see a growing emphasis on practical skills and project-based assessments, over rote learning or isolated tasks. Educators will continue to refine their techniques to balance content delivery with skill development, all while ensuring individual learning needs are not overlooked.

The world is moving away from the model of memorizing facts toward the importance of understanding and applying concepts. The aim is to prepare a generation of explorers, innovators, and global citizens who can navigate the complexities of our ever-expanding universe.

This transformation in astronomy education is not an overnight process. It is a considered evolution that requires commitment, creativity, and collaboration from all stakeholders - teachers, students, and our wider educational community. We are only on the brink of this exciting journey, with the cosmos as our frontier and knowledge as our guiding star.

To paraphrase Carl Sagan, we are just star-stuff exploring the stars. By embracing these dynamic pedagogical shifts, we ensure that each voyage into the depths of the universe is a shared journey, an adventure that ignites the imagination, fuels curiosity, and expands our collective understanding of the cosmos.

Chapter 3. The Evolution of Astronomy Instruction: A Historical Perspective

The understanding of celestial bodies and the universe has undergone several transformative changes, shaping teaching methods and strategies alike. The context of astronomy instruction seen today is the outcome of a fascinating history of evolution.

3.1. The Seeds of Astronomy in Ancient Times

The roots of astronomy sink deep into ancient civilizations. The Egyptians, Mayans, and the Chinese are revered as early astronomers, who observed the heavens not just for understanding the universe but also for practical applications such as keeping time and marking seasons. For these societies, the teaching of astronomy was largely confined to the elite and involved oral instruction and apprenticeship.

3.2. The Greeks and the Birth of Modern Astronomy

The Greek civilization, however, was the one to systematize the study of astronomy. Around 6th Century BC, noted philosopher Thales proposed theories that diverged from mythology and attempted at explaining celestial objects and events using rational thinking. Teaching astronomy then involved mentored study, interpreting established doctrines, and peer discussions.

In the Hellenistic Period, the likes of Hipparchus and Ptolemy built extensive catalogs of stars and made significant advancements in observational equipment. Libraries and learning centers, like the one at Alexandria, became critical repositories of this accumulated knowledge, providing an organisational backbone for more formalized instructions.

3.3. Middle Ages: Islamic Golden Age and the Revival of Astronomy

During the Middle Ages, when Europe grappled with the Dark Ages, Middle-Eastern scholars translated, preserved, and expanded upon the Greco-Roman astronomical knowledge during what is termed as the Islamic Golden Age. Academies like The House of Wisdom in Baghdad became hotspots for scientific discourse and educational endeavours, setting the stage for Arabic Numerals, trigonometry, and advancements in observational astronomy. This knowledge later percolated back into Europe, igniting a renaissance in learning and challenging established dogma.

3.4. The Renaissance and the Copernican Revolution

The Renaissance was a turning point in astronomy instruction, with scholarly work supported by increased literacy rates and the advent of the printing press. This period saw the Copernican Revolution that posited a heliocentric solar system, challenging the geocentric model that had long dominated academic and religious teachings. The following adversity and heated discussions led to a demarcation of science from religion, making room for empirical evidence and observation in understanding the universe.

3.5. The Enlightened Age and Modern Observational Astronomy

During the Age of Enlightenment in the 17th Century, the scientific method took root, with a newfound focus on evidence and reason, fostering innovations like Newtonian Physics and Kepler's laws of planetary motion. The telescope's innovative usage by Galileo Galilei ushered in the era of rigorous astronomical observation.

Teaching during this era remained mostly one-sided, with the professor delivering lectures and students passively taking notes. Practical learning in the field only became feasible with the proliferation of observatory use among astronomy students in the late 19th Century.

3.6. The 20th Century to Present: A Quantum Leap

The advent of the 20th Century brought a drastic shift in astronomy and its instruction, with the inception of quantum mechanics and Einstein's theory of relativity, fundamentally altering our understanding of the universe.

The prevalence of the World Wars saw a momentary halt in instruction, but the post-war period saw a resurgence with the Space Race. It sparked a wider interest in astronomy and led to an expansion in research, infrastructure, and ultimately teaching. This included the creation of planetariums designed to replicate the night sky, opening up access for urban dwellers and classrooms.

3.7. Astronomy Instruction in the Digital Age

The Digital Age has further revolutionized astronomy instruction. The internet has opened up vast resources and learning platforms for teachers and students, paving the way for interactive lesson plans and simulations, while distance learning has broken down geographical barriers.

Furthermore, the inception of collaboratively operated space observatories and advanced data processing software has allowed students to engage in hands-on research from early stages of their education. Astronomy has hence moved from being a passive learning experience to a more interactive, student-driven discipline.

One of the most significant shifts in the pedagogical approach has been the move towards collaborative learning. With a focus on peer interaction and group activities, this approach fosters critical thinking and decision-making skills. This shift prepares them for the real-world science, where collaboration and teamwork is the key to solving complex universal mysteries.

In summary, astronomy instruction has evolved through various stages - starting from the primitive observational reports in ancient times to the modern, tech-driven, collaborative instruction methodology. While the subject matter has always been captivating, it's the instructional strategies that have truly propelled our comprehension of the universe. As we gaze into the future of astronomy instruction, it promises to be as expansive and enthralling as the cosmos themselves.

Chapter 4. The Science and Art of Collaborative Learning

Collaborative learning, a pedagogical practice often relegated to niches of the humanities, is fast gaining traction in the field of astronomy. Pioneered by avant-garde educators, this approach breaks the bounds of traditional solitary learning, embracing the collective wisdom and diverse perspectives of students.

4.1. The Collaborative Learning Framework

The basis of collaborative learning is quite simple: learning as a group activity. This builds on Lev Vygotsky's Zone of Proximal Development theory, where students learn more effectively when in the company of peers. They can deliberate, question, explain and explore concepts together, giving rise to a richer understanding.

Traditionally, science and particularly astronomy have been subjects of independent research and study. However, this does not have to be the case—collaborative learning can be woven into this discipline with extraordinary effects. Educationally, students who are allowed to work collaboratively often arrive at solutions swiftly, strengthen their critical thinking skills, and have a more satisfactory learning experience.

Conceptual clarity in astronomy, a subject that relies heavily on abstract ideas and theories, can be challenging to achieve. However, when a group of learners brainstorms together, they simplify complex ideas through explanation, debate, and collective reasoning. This makes the subject more approachable and the learning more entrenched—thus successfully making a case for collaboration in astronomy education.

4.2. Implementing Collaborative Learning in Astronomy

Transforming a classroom into a cooperative learning environment isn't simply about grouping students together and hoping for the best. It requires precise planning, appropriate instructional strategies, and an openness to continuously tweak the process based on students' feedback. It may sound daunting, but the dividends in terms of enhanced learning are worth the effort.

One effective strategy is the 'jigsaw classroom' model, where students are divided into several groups tasked with understanding various aspects of a topic. After a set period, members from each group are regrouped to form new teams, where they impart the knowledge of their initial area of study. This encourages peer teaching and reinforces knowledge acquisition.

In the context of astronomy, one group could explore the life and death of stars while another delves into galaxy formations. In an ensuing meeting, a student explaining stellar evolution would gain a clearer understanding because of the necessity to present with coherence and simplicity. Similarly, the person learning also benefits, as the explanation comes from a peer, sometimes making it more relatable .

4.3. Collaborative Learning Technologies in Astronomy

The dawn of the digital era has broadened the prospects of collaborative learning in astronomy. A myriad of tools and technologies can facilitate communication and enhance interactive learning among students irrespective of geographic constraints. These revolutionary platforms help students collaborate in real-time, conduct virtual observations, and engage in data analysis collectively.

Online platforms like Slack, Google Classroom, and online whiteboards transform group study. These tools offer functionalities like real-time editing, discussion threads, and even virtual 'breakout rooms' for small group interactions. For observational astronomy, programs such as the Sloan Digital Sky Survey or Google Sky offer a wealth of tangible, real-world data that groups can explore and analyze together.

Aside from these, multi-player online games and virtual world simulations can make the learning experience engaging and fun. They offer a collaborative space, allowing students to navigate the universe, construct galaxies or simulate the life cycle of stars together. The Universe Sandbox and Stellarium are notable mentions in the catalog of astronomy-focused interactive platforms.

4.4. Challenges and Potential Solutions

Despite its promise, collaborative learning in astronomy is not without its hurdles. For the collaborative learning model to work, students' participation is key. However, some may hesitate to contribute due to fear of judgment or lack of confidence. Fostering a safe, non-judgmental environment is essential to counteract this. Success stories, encouraging feedback, and positive reinforcement can boost students' confidence and their willingness to participate in collective discussions.

Group dynamics is another challenge. A dominating member might stifle the voices of more reticent participants. To mitigate this, each group member can be assigned a specific role - presenter, note-taker, time-keeper, etc. This assures that everyone has a defined role and the group functions cohesively.

Embarking on the journey of collaborative astronomy education isn't easy. The road is riddled with challenges that warrant innovative solutions. However, the rewards of persistence are immense—a generation of astronomy students enriched with shared knowledge, honed critical thinking skills, and a deeper appreciation for the cosmos. Collaborative learning is more than just an instructional strategy; it's an exploration of the universe, done together. Through sharing, listening, and learning, we foster not only a new way of understanding but also the development and evolution of a thriving, curious community of young astronomers. Despite the distance between us and the stars, collaborative learning has the potential to bring the universe within our reach.

Chapter 5. Spotlight on Inclusive Pedagogy: Bringing Astronomy to Everyone

Astronomy, often dubbed as the oldest of sciences, offers a unique platform that can break down barriers and create opportunities for everyone to dive into the wonders of the universe. This journey of bringing astronomy to all is what we explore here.

5.1. The Essence of Inclusive Pedagogy

Inclusive pedagogy represents an ideology centered around creating teaching environments that cater to the learning needs of all students, irrespective of their diverse abilities, cultural backgrounds, or experiences. It's a method that seeks to remove the traditional boundaries often erected by the 'one size fits all' approach and instead create a student-centered learning experience.

In the context of astronomy, the application of this approach implies lessons which engage students at all knowledge levels, ensuring everyone can access and appreciate the complexities of the cosmos. This incorporation of every student's experience involves purposeful planning and delivery of teaching materials by the instructors. This also means employing innovative teaching methods, using cutting-edge technology, and creating an environment where diverse knowledge, perspectives, and experiences are valued equally.

5.2. The Shift Towards Inclusivity

For quite some time, astronomy was often viewed as an exclusive domain, reserved for the few. The intricate terminologies and complex mathematical equations often stonewalled the interest of the broader population, deterring many from venturing into this realm. However, the shift towards inclusive pedagogy has revolutionized how astronomy is taught.

This transformation subtly began with the recognition of the different talents, intelligences, and learning styles that students possess. Instructors started paying heed to the principles of Universal Design for Learning (UDL), a framework instrumental in creating equitable learning environments. These principles have been integrated into lesson planning, creating a multidimensional approach to teaching, set to engage and enthral every student in the classroom.

5.3. How Inclusive Pedagogy Works in an Astronomy Classroom

Let's consider an astronomy class in action, one designed around the tenets of inclusive pedagogy:

Imagine walking into a classroom where a vibrant 3-dimensional model of the solar system hangs down the ceiling. Soft instrumental music fills the air as students move about, inspecting the model, touching, sensing, and experiencing the complexity of the celestial bodies on display. The instructor moves amongst them, facilitating their learning journey, helping them connect their sensory perception with theoretical concepts. Occasionally, the room transforms into a space station, with role-playing activities in action, students analyzing real astronomical data, tinkering with telescope operations and much more. Here, everyone learns together, collaboratively, through active engagement.

5.4. Technology: A Catalyst for Inclusion

In the age of digital technology, innovative tools have played a significant role in shaping inclusive pedagogy in astronomy. From Virtual Reality (VR) headsets capable of transporting learners to the lunar surface, to powerful software enabling the creation of detailed star maps, technology has expanded the horizons of learning.

The utilization of these resources has made astronomy more accessible than ever. Visually impaired students have tactile 3-dimensional printed star maps at their disposal, and subtitles, sign language interpreters, and voice recognition software have opened up new learning avenues for hearing-impaired students. Inclusivity, thus, is no longer a luxury, but an attainable reality.

5.5. Breaking Down Cultural Barriers via Astronomy

Global diversity adds another level to the need for inclusivity. A truly inclusive astronomy class recognizes the cultural significance of celestial bodies across different traditions. Integrating these cultural narratives within the scientific framework can make learning more relatable and engaging for students from different cultural backgrounds.

For instance, the stories of constellations vary from culture to culture. Drawing parallels between these diverse celestial interpretations can inspire a sense of wonder and mutual respect amongst students.

5.6. Empowering Students: The Ultimate Goal

Ultimately, the aim of inclusive pedagogy in astronomy is to empower every student. By creating a learning environment that respects and values each student's unique skills and talents, we cultivate learners who appreciate the diversity of our universe just as they do the diversity amongst themselves. The astronomical classroom becomes a microcosm of the cosmos, illustrating that each individual, like each celestial body, holds a unique place and offers a unique perspective of the universe.

In closing, the transformation of astronomy lessons through inclusive pedagogy carries the promise of fostering a global appetite for astronomical learning. After all, the universe belongs to us all, and it's about time that we extend the same philosophy to learning about it. By continuing this journey towards inclusivity, we can look forward to a future where the wonders of the cosmos are accessible to everyone.

Chapter 6. Case Studies: Successful Collaborative Astronomy Programs

Our journey begins with the exploration of several key programs that have successfully adopted collaborative learning strategies in astronomy instruction, embodying the innovativeness and effectiveness that such approaches bring.

6.1. Sky Gazers: Marrying Hands-On Exploration with Teamwork

Sky Gazers is a locally-rooted program based in the rural Midwest that uses an inventive pedagogical model promoting learning through shared experiences. In their drive to make astronomy approachable and meaningful to their students, they've managed to transform their humble community observatory into a vibrant, community-led learning centre popular for its collaborative classes.

The program's success lies in its structure which couples theoretical learning with hands-on exploration. Students start with in-depth group discussions around a certain celestial body or phenomenon, supported with resources such as texts, audio-visual aids, and expert lectures. This theoretical inspection paves the way for a collective journey towards the observatory, where students together observe the celestial body, consolidating their learning in a real-world context.

From a quantitative perspective, Sky Gazers boasts of a high enrollment with student engagement levels spiking towards the end of each weeklong course. Anecdotal records recount how students have developed not only an appreciation for astronomy, but also valuable team-building skills and critical thinking abilities, underlying the effectiveness of collaborative learning.

6.2. Star Trackers: Leveraging Technology for Collaborative Learning

In contrast to our previous case, Star Trackers is a digitally-driven program, illustrating that collaborative astronomy education can thrive in a virtual environment. Formed in response to the widespread disruption of face-to-face learning due to the 2020 pandemic, the program serves as a prime example of resilient, technology-enabled collaborative education.

The online platform hosts a variety of interactive activities, including virtual stargazing events, collaborative research projects, discussions, and problem-solving activities around cosmological phenomena. Unique to Star Trackers is their innovative use of gamified learning elements, where students work together to solve complex space-themed puzzles or collaboratively construct intricate models of celestial bodies, encouraging active learning and engagement.

Web analytics depict a steady rise in student involvement with consistent interactions taking place even outside designated class hours. This program has not only demystified the cosmos to its student body, but also evolved into a tight-knit online community of astronomy enthusiasts fostering camaraderie and knowledge exchange.

6.3. Cosmos Conquerors: Cross-Institutional Collaboration

Cosmos Conquerors takes collaboration to a higher level by partnering with various academic institutions to offer an immersive, project-based learning experience. Students from diverse academic backgrounds collaborate to design and execute astronomy-related experiments, tapping into the synergies their varied skillsets generate.

In these multicentric collaborations, students communicate remotely, exchanging ideas, data, and updates, culminating their project in a joint presentation. The program also employs the expertise of mentors from partnered institutions, enriching student experiences with professional insights and technical knowledge.

Over the past years, Cosmos Conquerors has seen a multitude of projects come to fruition—ranging from designing space weather predicting models to building efficient telescopes. End-of-course feedback consistently lauds the program for enhancing students' interpersonal and research skills and nurturing their curiosity for the universe, demonstrating the synergistic effect when collaboration stretches across institutions.

Our examination of these markedly different yet successful programs brings forward the versatility and capability of collaborative learning frameworks when applied to astronomy instruction. It's encouraging to observe the rise in such initiatives, reiterating the shifting paradigm towards co-learning in pursuit of unraveling the secrets of the cosmos. The onward journey for astronomical education looks promisingly star-studded, illuminated with the shared enthusiasm and inquisitiveness of learners and educators alike.

Chapter 7. New Tools for Engagement: Technology in Modern Astronomy Education

As we pivot towards a more collaborative learning approach with astronomy instruction, the role of technology as an engagement tool is increasingly crucial. Not only does it provide fresh ways of access and interaction with vast cosmic knowledge but also the means to foster healthy learning collaborations.

7.1. The Leverage of Digital Technology

In the era of the digital revolution, data management and manipulation have become increasingly important. Astronomy, being a data-rich subject, greatly benefits from digital technology. For instance, online databases like SIMBAD, NED, and ADS facilitate astronomers in finding data about stars, galaxies, and other celestial bodies. These databases, frequently updated with data from worldwide observations, afford students the chance to engage with and manipulate real-time cosmic data—an unprecedented opportunity that can heighten learning interest and participation.

Moreover, data visualization tools are emerging as essentials in astronomy education, allowing students to comprehend complex spatial relationships and patterns. Software such as WorldWide Telescope, Celestia, and Google Sky presents students with interactive 3D models of celestial bodies, enabling the understanding of concepts that are difficult to teach through traditional methods.

Thus, digital technology can powerfully expand the reach of astronomy education, transforming the learning experience from inherently solitary into a dynamic and engaging process.

7.2. Adaptive Learning Systems

Adaptive learning systems harness the power of artificial intelligence to personalize learning experiences based on individual students' knowledge level and learning pace. These tools adapt in real time to student performance, adjusting the level of challenge and providing feedback to ensure comprehension.

For astronomy education, adaptive learning systems can revolutionize the way complex concepts and processes are understood, providing modules that adapt based on student answers. They can reinforce learning through repetition, drill-style exercises, and gamified solutions, making the learning process more interactive and enjoyable.

7.3. Virtual and Augmented Reality

Incorporating virtual reality (VR) and augmented reality (AR) can make the universe more accessible to students, offering immersive experiences that transform the learning environment. With VR, learners can embark on tours of distant galaxies or observe Earth from the International Space Station. At the same time, AR can overlay information on physical models, enhancing traditional learning tools.

Applications such as "Universe Sandbox" and "SkyView" amalgamate visuals and physics to materialize dynamic astronomical events that occur over long time spans in an accelerated time frame. Consequently, learners can foster a deep understanding of these distant astronomical processes, which are impossible to observe in real-life conditions.

VR and AR also enable collaborative explorations of the cosmos, facilitating a community learning experience, and instigating introspective dialogues about the universe and our place within it.

7.4. Online Collaborative Spaces

Advancements in network technology have birthed online collaborative environments where students can share their insights, work in groups, and aid peers in solving problems. Platforms like Google Workspace, Slack, and Microsoft Teams, while initially utilized for business communication, have witnessed increased adoption in education scenarios.

Collaborative documents and video conferencing tools support remote learning programs, allowing educators and students to connect from different locations. Simultaneously, shared digital whiteboards provide learners an opportunity to collaboratively brainstorm, sketch concepts, and critique one another's work in real-time.

Learners can also tap social media platforms with educational thrusts. For example, students can follow NASA or other space exploration agencies on Twitter, keeping them abreast with recent discoveries and developments, and enabling an informed conversation.

In a nutshell, these technologies have made possible a powerful convergence of astronomy, education, and collaboration, creating a vibrant, stimulating environment that is likely to inspire a new generation of astronomers.

7.5. Challenges and the Way Forward

Despite the promising evolution, technology in astronomy education also presents challenges. For instance, a significant digital divide still exists across regions, potentially excluding some learners from these innovative pedagogies. Hence, educators and policymakers must develop solutions to ensure inclusive digital access.

Similarly, integrating technology in traditional classrooms demands a paradigm shift in teaching methodologies and considerable investment in infrastructure, professional development, and tech support.

On the educational front, while technology can capture interest and aid in understanding complex concepts, it can also become a distraction if not adequately managed. The careful design of learning activities and guidelines for appropriate tech usage are thus necessary.

The future of astronomy education is luminous with collaboration and technology at its core. As we step forward into this new education era, we must tackle these challenges head-on, ensuring that all students—not just the economically and geographically privileged—get the opportunity to explore the cosmos through these exciting new windows of knowledge. Let these new tools for engagement in modern astronomy education unfold the infinite universe in ways we've never before conceived!

Chapter 8. From Solo Observation to Group Discovery: A Cultural Shift

In astronomy instruction, think back to the traditional image: a lone figure, head tilted skyward, peering into the vastness of the celestial sphere. Armed with a telescope, their objective was to decipher the enigmatic patterns of stars and celestial bodies. This solitary pursuit, however, is being increasingly replaced by one that promotes camaraderie, fostering a learning environment where discovery is a shared endeavor. The movement from solo observation to group discovery represents a significant cultural shift in the instruction of astronomy.

8.1. The Lone Observer: A Historical Perspective

In the annals of astronomy, individuals working in isolation have made incredible discoveries. From Galileo Galilei in the 17th century to contemporary physicists like Stephen Hawking, astronomy has a long history of solitary observers probing the cosmos. These singular minds, armed with telescopes and theories, have unraveled many of the universe's secrets.

But why this trend towards solo observation? There are two main reasons. First, the complexity of astronomical calculations and observations once demanded an intense focus only achievable in solitude. Second, access to astronomical instruments, such as telescopes, was often limited to a lucky few.

8.2. Rising Collaborative Trend: An Overview

Yet the tide has been turning towards more collaborative methods in recent years. In this shift, the image of individual seekers of celestial knowledge has been enhanced by a collective of inquiring minds, engaged in a communal quest for understanding.

This trend has received a boost from advancements in technology and pedagogical shifts. With the advent of digital technology and remote sensing equipment, astronomical data can now be shared, discussed, and questioned by an interdisciplinary team of learners. They can collectively interpret the cosmos, debating and refining their theories in a mutually supportive environment.

8.3. The Cultural Shift: Factors for Transformation

At the heart of this new approach are three catalysts: accessibility, plurality, and toolkit augmentation. First, the proliferation of accessible technology has democratized astronomical observation. With remote-operated telescopes and online databases, astronomy no longer demands exclusivity.

Next is the emergence of the plurality perspective. When learners from diverse backgrounds and with varied skills work together on a single project, they bring unique inputs to the analysis of findings. Ideas converge, diffuse, and re-assemble, enhancing the understanding of both learning and natural phenomena.

The third factor, toolkit augmentation, comes from the expansion of the research tools available to the average student or group. Machine learning, data analysis software, and virtual reality can now all be brought to bear in the field of astronomy education. These tools not only increase the capacity to make new discoveries but also enhance the interactive and collaborative aspect of learning.

8.4. Group Observation in Practice

Group observations today take many forms, from collaborative analysis sessions to group stargazing events. Students might band together to tackle complex astronomical problems or collectively trawl through vast swaths ⁄ of data. Web-forums and online communities facilitate discussion about celestial bodies and phenomena, allowing learners from across the globe to interact and learn from each other.

In one renowned example, students participating in the Online Astronomy Project – a collaborative research initiative – made a genuine discovery: they identified an asteroid. Revelations such as these prove that collaboration can yield tangible results and provide students with an unparalleled sense of achievement.

8.5. The Impact of Collaboration

The collective approach to discovery has a transformative effect on learning. It fosters a sense of shared responsibility among learners, instills a deeper understanding of concepts as they explain and discuss them with others, and nurtures creativity by encouraging different perspectives and approaches.

Furthermore, this collaborative learning experience captures students' imaginations, inspires them, and motivates them to participate actively, which increases their engagement with the subject matter. It transforms astronomy from a passive reception of knowledge to an active creation of understanding.

8.6. Looking to the Future

This shift from solo observation toward group discovery is likely to continue gaining momentum. As technological innovations keep lowering the barriers to access, and educators prioritize active, collaborative learning, the future of astronomy education is looking increasingly bright and profound.

In a world where scientific problems are ever more complex and interconnected, an interdisciplinary, multifaceted approach to learning is no longer just beneficial; it's essential. The move from solo observation to group discovery embodies this evolution, inculcating in students a deep reverence for the mysteries of the cosmos and the exciting journey of discovery they undertake—together.

Chapter 9. Involving the Larger Community: The Interdisciplinary Potential of Astronomy

The fertile ground for astronomical knowledge proliferates beyond the traditional pedestal of a classroom. By extending the realms of understanding, the rich and vast domain of astronomy can be integrated into a larger community. The application of such an interdisciplinary approach can result in the unfurling of a galaxy of potential within the fields of art, history, culture, and even philosophy. The inherent synergy derived from such intersectionality can prove to be a catalyst for lively debate, intellectual growth, and holistic learning experiences.

9.1. Inroads into the Artistic Universe

We often venerate the night sky as the silent muse for numerous artistic creations. Unsurprisingly, the bridge between astronomy and art is built on the profound awe and curiosity that the cosmos inspires. The potentiality to toggle between the contrasting yet complimentary realms of logic and creativity opens doors to innumerable possibilities. A project-based approach could involve students in creating art that manifests their understanding of celestial events. This method provides an alternative yet effective form to probe into the mysteries of the universe without being too entrenched in scientific jargon.

Photo exhibitions showcasing the treasures of the cosmos, contests to design infographics on astronomical phenomena, or creating "sounds of space" through musical interpretation can all be valuable contributors to the learning journey open to a larger audience.

9.2. History's Celestial Chronicles

Historically, astronomy has served as a significant intellectual premise for several ancient civilizations. Knowledge from these celestial observations seeped into their calendars, agriculture, and prediction of seasonal changes. A close integration of history and astronomy can allow students to delve deep into examining the societal influence of astronomical events through various epochs of human civilization.

Structured discussions on how phenomena such as solar eclipses, comets, supernovae, or the understanding of the celestial sphere influenced societal beliefs and behaviors can encourage students to appreciate the omnipotence of the cosmos and its perennial impact on our forebearers.

9.3. Cultural Constellations

Astronomy, laden with its inerrant marvels, effortlessly seeps through the fabric of diverse cultures and forms an essential part of folklore, mythology, and tribal customs. The intertwining of astronomy and culture opens up a diverse learning experience, where students can explore celestial interpretations from the vantage point of different cultures.

Role-play, storytelling, or even creating a cultural event celebrating astronomical events can significantly enhance the understanding of how celestial occurrences seep into the intimate corners of our human existence, reflecting universal appeal and fascination with the cosmos.

9.4. Philosophical Pathways Through the Cosmos

"Man is a microcosm, or a little world, because he is an extract from all the stars and planets" - Paracelsus. This quote exemplifies how astronomy and philosophy forge an unlikely yet profound alliance. By venturing into the abstract realms of existential questions, students can be drawn into contemplating the enormity of the universe and humanity's relative insignificance.

Philosophical debates based on astronomical theories and discoveries can engage students in thought-provoking discussions, potentially offering a deeper, more nuanced perspective on the universe. Topics could include the existence of extraterrestrial life, the idea of multiple universes, or the philosophical implications of black holes.

9.5. Creating Collaborative Synergy

The intrinsic potential of interdisciplinary learning in astronomy can be realized only if we skillfully orchestrate a proactive exchange of ideas across various disciplines. Collaboration with local artists, historians, cultural organizations, and even philosophers can provide opportunities for expansive dialogue and learning.

Creating an open platform for sharing knowledge, hosting lecture series by experts from different walks of life, or organizing community events to discuss the impact of celestial phenomena on different levels of society, all harness the potential of the larger community to enrich the learning experience significantly.

Ultimately, by placing astronomy at the crux of an interdisciplinary educational approach, we can tap into a universal fascination with the cosmos. This not only enhances intellectual growth across different dimensions but also provides a unique pedagogical tool to encourage curiosity, creativity and a sense of communal learning experience.

Chapter 10. Implementation Challenges: Overcoming Obstacles in Collaborative Learning

The shift towards collaborative learning in astronomy instruction requires substantial effort from educators, but it is not without challenges. Implementing this strategy successfully demands rigorous curriculum development, thoughtful facilitation, and a supportive environment that cultivates student participation and teamwork. At the same time, the dynamic and unpredictable nature of collaborative learning comes with a unique set of obstacles that educators need to overcome, which we detail below.

10.1. Defining Clear Goals

One of the first challenges in implementing collaborative learning is formulating clear and achievable goals. Unlike traditional lecture-based teaching methods, collaborative learning requires a high degree of student involvement and interaction. It is essential, therefore, for educators to outline explicit objectives at the start of each session, which can create a sense of purpose and direction. Without specific goals, students may lose focus, leading to decreased participation and ineffective collaboration.

Establishing these goals is not without obstacles. Educators may struggle to strike a balance between creating a challenging yet attainable target. Furthermore, these goals need to be devised in a way that encourages collective effort rather than individual competition. Tools like interactive mind maps and shared documents can aid in the process, fostering clear communication and mutual understanding of the project objectives.

10.2. Cultivating a Collaborative Culture

Creating an effective collaborative learning environment necessitates a shift in the conventional educational culture. Students and teachers alike need to adjust their mindset to one that values cooperation, mutual respect, and openness. Developing such a culture can be a complex task, as it requires overcoming engrained habits of competition and solitary work.

In classroom settings, educators can promote a cooperative atmosphere by emphasizing the importance of every student's contribution and encouraging inclusive discussions. Training in conflict resolution can also be beneficial, as conflict is an inevitable part of collaborative processes. Handling disagreements in a constructive manner and turning them into learning opportunities can significantly enhance the effectiveness of collaborative learning.

10.3. Adapting to Diverse Learning Styles

Collaborative learning brings together diverse groups of students, each with their unique learning style. Some students may prefer hands-on activities and experiments, while others may learn better through discussions or independent research. Adapting teaching strategies to accommodate these individual preferences can be a challenging hurdle for educators.

One potential solution is to use mixed learning strategies during collaborative sessions. By alternating between experiential, observational, and theoretical methods, educators can cater to a wide range of learning styles. This variety can also contribute to keeping the sessions engaging and dynamic.

10.4. Managing Group Dynamics

Group dynamics play a significant role in the success of collaborative learning. Bad chemistry between team members or unequal participation could hinder learning progress. Managing group dynamics effectively requires keen observational skills and the ability to intervene constructively when issues arise.

Strategies for effective group management include creating clear roles within groups, facilitating open communication, and promoting shared responsibility. Team building exercises can also be helpful to foster positive group dynamics.

10.5. Evaluating Individual Contributions

Evaluating individual contributions within a collaborative learning setting can be difficult but is necessary for fair assessment. It may be challenging to discern the input of each student in a group task, and students might feel their work is not accurately represented. However, using peer assessment methods, detailed group logs and individual reflective journals can help in capturing students' contributions effectively.

10.6. Integrating Technology

In today's era, technology integration is a vital part of modern education, including collaborative learning in astronomy instruction. However, identifying appropriate technologies and platforms that enhance collaboration, and training all students to use these tools, can be daunting tasks.

From shared online workspaces to virtual reality headsets for celestial exploration, educators must choose appropriate tools based on their specific needs and resources. In addition, educators need to ensure that all students have equal access to these technologies to maintain fairness and inclusivity.

In conclusion, implementing collaborative learning in astronomy instruction is not a simple task due to the challenges it presents. However, through careful planning, innovative strategies, and persistent effort, educators can overcome these issues and foster a rewarding collaborative learning environment. Be prepared to face the challenges head-on with patience, creativity, and resilience, and remember that the rewarding outcome – more engaged, motivated, and collaborative students – is well worth the effort.

Chapter 11. Looking Ahead: The Future of Collaborative Astronomy Instruction

In the ever-evolving field of astronomy instruction, integral changes are incorporating aspects of collaborative learning. More than ever, teamwork and shared experiences are seen as key factors in fostering a deeper understanding of the cosmos. But what does the future look like for such an exciting merger of traditional science instruction and novel, interactive learning strategies? Let's delve in and discover the remarkable potential ahead.

11.1. Collaboration Stations

One of the most significant shifts in contemporary astronomy education involves creating interaction-oriented study environments dubbed as 'Collaboration Stations.' Here, students congregate in physical or digital spaces, tackling specific celestial study topics through team exercises and projects. These environments ardently foster 21st-century skills, such as digital literacy, creativity, problem-solving, and communication skills. Providing a platform for peer-driven, organic learning, these Spaces are quickly becoming a favored pedagogical method for astronomy instruction.

11.2. Incorporating AI and Machine Learning Tools

Artificial intelligence and machine learning tools will play an increasingly significant role in advancing collaborative astronomy instruction. Not solely a shortcut to data analysis, AI-infused tools encourage collaborative exploration of massive datasets and complex computational astronomy. They have the capacity to bring observatory-quality data directly to the classroom, enabling students to be part of pioneering research. With these tools, students transition from being passive receivers of knowledge into proactive scientific investigators.

Exploration of AI-enhanced virtual laboratories, where students can operate advanced equipment remotely, is another promising development. This offers an authentic experience of cutting-edge scientific practice while enabling international collaboration between educators and students—making research and discovery a shared endeavor.

11.3. Immersive Technologies: VR and AR

Virtual and Augmented Reality (VR and AR) technology have the ability to transport students to any location in the universe, providing immersive educational experiences that deeply engage and inspire. For example, VR planetariums can offer educational experiences previously limited to large and costly traditional planetariums.

As the technology becomes more accessible and integrated, students collaborating in real-time across the globe through VR/AR will become commonplace. These technologies will extend learning beyond classroom boundaries—allowing students to work collaboratively on simulations of space missions, exploration of celestial bodies, and more.

11.4. Open-Source Learning Resources

In the near future, we can anticipate a surge of open-source, high-quality, student-centered astronomy curriculum materials. These resources, covering a broad spectrum of topics and inquiries, facilitate collaboration and active learning.

This includes massive online open courses (MOOCs), digital textbooks incorporating multimedia, and interactive Star Maps. Open platforms will encourage active participation—allowing students to add content, discuss theories with experts, peer review work, and share their projects.

11.5. Citizen Science Projects

Citizen science projects will become an increasingly prevalent part of collaborative astronomy instruction. By engaging students in real research projects, we can provide them with authentic scientific experiences and make them part of the global scientific community. These projects inspire, while also teaching scientific methodology, critical analysis, collaboration, and peer review skills.

11.6. Continued Professional Development for Educators

In this innovative educational landscape, continued professional development for astronomy educators will be essential. As the methodologies evolve and new technologies come to the fore, teacher training programs will need to incorporate these innovations.

This includes training to effectively use AI and machine learning tools, VR and AR technology, and advice on forming collaborative environments. Ensuring educators are comfortable with these new approaches will smooth the transition and ensure synchrony between student learning and the wider educational strategy.

11.7. Final Words: An Internationally Collaborative Future

Combining collaboration and modern tools, future astronomy instruction has the promise of creating global classrooms. These classrooms will extend their boundaries beyond geographical barriers. United by a shared curiosity, students will collaboratively piece together puzzles about our universe—extending our understanding of the cosmos.

This new landscape of space instruction already shimmering on the horizon, is not just possible—it's inevitable. With these advancements, the implications for education, for science, and for our sense of human connectedness across the globe, are as vast and impressive as the cosmos itself.

www.ingramcontent.com/pod-product-compliance
Lightning Source LLC
LaVergne TN
LVHW051626050326
832903LV00033B/4684